COME BACK TO LOVE

Understandings and Reflections on Self-Love

Elsa Mendoza

Copyright © 2019 Elsa Mendoza

All rights reserved.

This publication may not be reproduced, stored in a retrieval system, or transmitted in whole or in part, in any form or by any means, electronic, mechanical, photocopying, recording, or otherwise, without the prior written permission of the author. This publication is designed to provide accurate and authoritative information in regard to the subject matter covered. It is sold with the understanding that the publisher is not engaged in rendering legal, accounting, or other professional service. If legal advice or other expert assistance is required, the services of a competent professional service should be sought.

Paperback ISBN: 9781070783055
Hardcover ISBN: 9781735686127

INTRODUCTION

No one is exempt from pain and suffering. Everyone has his own experience of despair and loneliness and everyone also transforms through these experiences. Some change for the better and some for the worse.

Each one of us is wired differently and shaped by our programming and beliefs. Everyone sees the physical world according to his lens. Every person is at a different level of awareness of life's events, especially the awareness of the self. There is an incessant search for one's self.

The lack of self-knowledge leads to more suffering and separation, especially in relationships. Everybody wants to be happy and to be loved. Sometimes one falls in love and enters relationships for the wrong reasons and expectations. Most of us think we are separate from one another and the Divine Source. We think love is outside of us. We have forgotten our true higher selves, our inner being, and so we are in a continuous search for it in different places, situations, and people. We also believe we are imperfect and incomplete beings, thus the said results and cycle.

Some make sense of themselves with the illogical, egoistic desires due to a mindset that perceives they lack in many things. These desires are: the need to have more, to compete, to be right, to be different, to be noticed, and to win. Others unknowingly yearn for control and conflict. We think we can and already know the essence of ourselves based on our successes, achievements, and acquisitions yet still feel empty and unloved. We are barely scratching the surface of our true powerful selves. Our emotions have consumed and mastered us, instead of our mastering our emotions.

However, there is already a shift of consciousness taking place in humanity. We have enough experiences of pain and suffering in this world that we clamor for change. We know that change should start within ourselves. Almost everyone is talking about self-love. The world needs more love, but love has to be realized, and it starts with loving ourselves.

This book is the expanded version of a poem from my second book, *Wake Up Humanity*. It is about self-love. I share with you the lessons and wisdom I learned and applied in my journey to self-love. If you open and allow yourself to receive and believe, it will answer your questions: what self-love means, how to love yourself more, and the effects of self-love. At the end of each topic, you will find questions to help you in your reflection. You will also find me using terms like God, Divine Source, Source, and Infinite Creator as this book is not catered to any specific belief. This book is special because of people's contributions on defining what love is based on their individual experiences.

There is always a way to change your challenging situation and it is with LOVE; a love that empowers and changes your life and everyone else's around you. This is SELF-LOVE. This is beyond pampering yourself a few hours each day, indulging in material possessions, telling yourself "I love you" in front of the mirror, and engaging in a challenge to love yourself within a specific timeframe.

You are invited to pause, reflect, and focus on how you have perceived and treated yourself for the past years. My only intention is to inspire and not to make grandiose claims. Self-help books are available for your guidance and reference. I have no desire to dictate what you need to do and I am not trying to proselytize to you. The decision is always up to you, and the answers that serve you have always been within you. You are free to find the truth that works for you.

It took years of moment-to-moment self-exploration and realization for me to understand self-love and eventually write this book. The message of this book is simple; self-love is essential as it affects your life, humanity, other sentient beings, and our world. Please read this book with an open mind and heart.

Peace, blessings, and love,

Elsa Mendoza, CCC
Long Beach, CA

DEDICATION

I lovingly dedicate this book to
those who want to establish a better
and loving relationship with themselves.

Contents

INTRODUCTION	i
DEDICATION	v
CHAPTER ONE: WHY I WROTE THIS BOOK	1
CHAPTER TWO: WHAT IS LOVE?	9
CHAPTER THREE: THE JOURNEYS TO SELF-LOVE	21
THE JOURNEY OF SELF-DISCOVERY/INTROSPECTION	*25*
THE JOURNEY OF SELF-ACCEPTANCE	*41*
THE JOURNEY OF SELF-FORGIVENESS AND SELF-UNDERSTANDING	*49*
THE JOURNEY OF SELF-HEALING/SELF-CARE	*53*
CHAPTER FOUR: UNDERSTANDING SELF-LOVE	63
CHAPTER FIVE: THE SELF-LOVE EFFECT	77
SELF-LOVE	*81*

REQUEST	83
ACKNOWLEDGEMENTS	85
ABOUT THE AUTHOR	87
ALSO BY ELSA MENDOZA	89
CONNECT WITH THE AUTHOR	91
RESOURCES	93

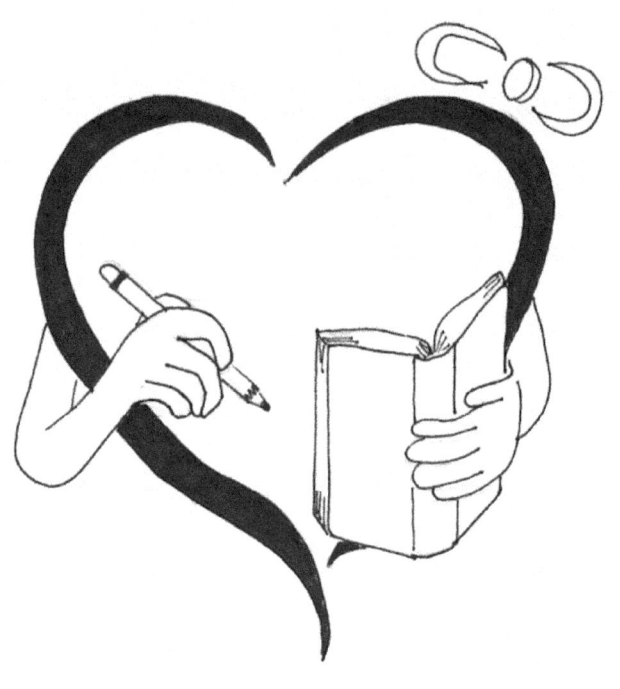

CHAPTER ONE
WHY I WROTE THIS BOOK

Everyone has a unique story to tell, and everyone has an experience that gave him or her a choice whether to live like a victim or to live like a champion. I share some of my actual life experiences, as I believe it can bring more inspiration, insight, motivation, and empowerment to you.

And my story goes like this: I came from a family where tough love was experienced. Growing up, my parents would beat up my siblings and me to discipline us. I felt unloved and thought to myself that love is not supposed to hurt. I would sit inside the corner of my parents' closet after the beatings, and there I would cry my heart out to God.

Part of my routine was to count the bruises on my body from the physical beatings from the early age of five until my early twenties. It was a violent and painful childhood. People look at my family as closely knit just because we lived under one roof. It may look ideal from the outside, but we needed help on the inside.

There were so much pain and suffering in the family, none of us could handle our personal struggles. We did not realize that every member of the family needed help to understand and love oneself first. There was no personal space to breathe. Bickering resulted in separation. Being the youngest in the family, I had to remove myself from that situation and find healing for myself. I left my family and country for work, which led me to understand more about myself and about love. In hindsight, I realized that my journey to self-love started the moment I removed myself from the toxic environment. Years back, I would tell this story from a victim's perspective and now I could only tell it as an inspired being. This foundation and experience became my motivation to live a life of peace, joy, and love.

You might have heard people talking about Near-Death Experiences or NDE, where they claimed to see a bright light, a presence of light, or a Divine Entity. It was January 2008 when I experienced the same thing. I recall that afternoon when I was rushed to the hospital because of difficulty in breathing, weakness, and bruising all over my body. Upon arrival in the hospital, I fell unconscious. During this state, I saw myself walking in the hallway of my apartment. The shade of light on the ceiling was the usual soft white color. The short stretch of the hallway to my bedroom became longer. I was walking in slow motion. As I walked to my bedroom, the soft white light color got brighter and brighter. As I got closer to the light, I felt the energy of pure ecstasy and bliss; and then I felt something more . . . more love. I was so mesmerized that all I wanted was to continue walking closer and stay in that experience forever. However, I heard someone call my name and realized I was lying on the floor surrounded by people in navy blue scrubs. One was holding my left wrist tightly, and I heard a firm voice say, "She's got a pulse!" I was conscious again, and someone scooped me up from the floor, carried me on a stretcher, and wheeled me to the ER. I learned that I was unconscious for about a minute. After that NDE, their diagnosis was Aplastic Anemia.

There are no words to recount how I felt during that experience. Love was just the closest word I could use to describe it. This experience was a revelation and confirmation for me: I am loved no matter what. It removed all my fears about death and about a judgmental and punishing image of God that I was taught to believe in. There's really nothing to fear, as it's just all LOVE. This started my spiritual journey where I was awakened from the "self" that I thought I knew. The soul spoke, and I heard it loud and clear. My perception of God, death, life, and myself has changed. It was a rebirth.

Looking back at these experiences, I realized that I have not fully understood how to love myself. I thought I could only experience love from external sources. I have forgotten who I truly am and, most especially, I have not grasped the love of the Divine Source for me. I have reached my lowest times, felt alone, empty, but was never damaged. There was this consistent stillness, awareness, and power from my core that kept me whole despite my circumstances and empowered me to rise, survive, and thrive. It was love from the Divine Source/Infinite Perfect Creator/God within me . . . the love that is also me. I am **only loved** and **not judged** by the same God.

These epiphanies started my spiritual awakening and led me to be the person I am today, in honor, appreciation, respect, and love for myself. I came to realize that I had to experience my lowest times to know my powerful self. Now I can also say those formidable moments with my family were the best thing that ever happened. The past didn't define me but only refined me. The ego-driven and self-playing victim was left enfeebled, and so my powerful loving self arose. Calmness and harmony came after the stormy experiences in my life. Love and peace tethered me back to my soul. At last, it is well with my soul.

I went through the journey of **Self-Discovery/Introspection, Self-Acceptance, Self-Forgiveness/Understanding,** and **Self-Healing/Self-Care** that all led to **Self-Love.** These journeys taught and showed me how to love myself. Please know that these journeys are continuous as we are in a life of eternal creation and contrast in this physical world conceptualized by our mind. We constantly encounter the positive and negative experiences in life, through our chosen beliefs, derived from our repetitive thoughts. These experiences can teach and help us in our evolution. Let me invite you again to listen to the nudges and whispers of your soul. Every moment is a moment of inspiration. Remember and rediscover the real you. The more you remember, the more you know that you are love-d. Ask for wisdom and guidance, be open to receiving, believing, and creating a life worth living.

REFLECTION:

What is your life-changing story?

How did it change you?

What propelled you to change?

What have you realized and learned?

How are you living your lessons and realizations?

CHAPTER TWO

WHAT IS LOVE?

Love is colossal. No words can really define love as it is immeasurable. Love is deep, so deep I can only say it is naked, boundless, and limitless. It is the absence of the egoistic "self." Each one of us has a different perspective on love. It can be a sensitive or complex subject to some. But what is love really? I asked a few people to help me define love, and it was the best part of writing this chapter. Through their definitions, I've known and appreciated them more. Like I have mentioned in the introduction of this book, my intention was to inspire, but it turned out I was the one who got more inspired! There is so much beauty in every soul. I believe that you will relate to some of them.

First, let me include a definition of love by Albert Einstein. I resonated strongly with it and I know you will, too. Einstein defined love in his letter to his daughter as:

"An extremely powerful force that, so far, science has not found a formal explanation to. It is a force that

includes and governs all others, and is even behind any phenomenon operating in the universe and has not yet been identified by us. This universal force is LOVE. When scientists looked for a unified theory of the universe, they forgot the most powerful unseen force. Love is Light that enlightens those who give and receive it. Love is gravity, because it makes some people feel attracted to others. Love is power, because it multiplies the best we have, and allows humanity not to be extinguished in their blind selfishness. Love unfolds and reveals. For love we live and die. Love is God and God is Love. This force explains everything and gives meaning to life. This is the variable that we have ignored for too long, maybe because we are afraid of love because it is the only energy in the universe that man has not learned to drive at will."

Einstein's definition of love got me wondering if it's the summation of humanity's current situation. What do you think?

Here are the definitions of love by the people who promptly and gladly took the time to respond to my request. I had an "aha" moment—you can know more about a person by asking what love is.

"It is all there is." – Qat Wanders

"It is everything." – Pam Jael

"It is kindness." – Jewel Sarmiento

"It is forgiveness." – Jennifer A. Paras

"It is caring." – Ndeye Labadens

"It is to know someone." – Karl Roger Melby

"It is the greatest gift of all." – Florence Rivera

"It is synonymous with selflessness." – Leileen Aniban

"It is not how much you say I love you." – Lea Dominguez

"It is kind, compassionate, and forgiving." – Veronica Wilken

"It is unconditional and your source of happiness." – Mary Antonette Torres

"It is the seed of transcendence and the ultimate remedy." – Lucky Starzinsky

"It is the infinite mystery and mastery of the Perfect Creator." – Meredith Swift

"It is a beautiful emotion we should all experience most often." – Maria Buch

"It is about care, support and selflessness. Love is about we and not I." – EB Sawaneh

"It is a feeling of happiness and contentment with yourself and your loved one." – Dennis Mendoza

"It cannot be easily defined as I can only feel it like the air I breathe and I can't live without it." – Beth Mathay

"It is self-sacrificing." – Noemi Victorino

"It is giving all my attention and time for my parents and kids as they're my top priority and my life." – Cris Ibarra

"It is selfless and putting the happiness of those I love before mine." – Gloria Jayona

"It is a sacrifice just like Jesus, He sacrificed His life just to save us and it is the love for God." – Analin Parocha

"It is being concerned with what benefits or makes a loved one convenient or happy." – Lourdes V. Lim

"It is when you give compassion, care, respect, consideration and all other virtues unconditionally to someone." – Ferdinand Moncada (LA's singing Makeup Artist)

"It is an unconditional act of constant selflessness. Although it may not be felt at all times, it should be able to be seen." – Ariston CM

"It is the most powerful miracle that God created and consider yourself lucky if you experience the beauty of it." – Ren Gulle

"It's that expansive feeling that leaves nothing or no one out of our heart." – Geeta Rao

"It is the strongest caring emotion ever created by a loving God." – Jill Young Rogers

"It is a humongous word, lots of wonderful meaning you can attached with it. Love is also pain." – Anonymous

*"It is a special feeling shared by two different people. It is the greatest gift of all. Love is love."
— Tess Diaz*

"It is not turning a blind eye to one's fault. It is letting the other person know his/her faults and shortcomings to change for the better thus bettering the relationship too." – Ency Cruz

"It is about self-love, which means self-respect and having standards. When you respect yourself, you won't allow disrespect from others. Having standards is what you will allow or not allow in your life." – Marlene Wagner

"It is 500 level consciousness that is a mid vibrational range in the spectrum that is the only downfall as it creates attachments that are barriers to enlightenment consciousness level." – Holly Yandle

"It is the act of opening the mind and heart to everything that goes with your subject that includes the good and the not so great, and going deeper to understand and accept and setting the ego aside. It's not about me anymore." – Cheryl Lisa (@thetalking_cat)

"It is unconditional, accepting people whole-heartedly for who and what they are, their flaws no matter what, and not expecting them to change for you. It is supporting people in all aspects of their lives in any way you can." – Razel Vicente

"It is the love of a mother for her child which is a perfect example of what love is. When your child's need is more important than yours. Love is selfless. Love is not easy, but the rewards are infinite." – Maria Teresa Silvestre

"It is removing the walls and offering forgiveness. It's letting go of your ego and opening your heart. It is caring for someone more than you thought possible and fighting for them when times get tough. It is indefinite." – Jennifer Walters

"It is the unconditional feeling, emotion, sense that compels us to want the very best at every level (mind, body, and spirit) for those that we do love." – Kathleen Quinton

"It comes in different forms: for oneself, another human being, animal, and inanimate objects. It makes somebody jump for joy and it can be hurtful, too. Love cannot be defined by book. It is an experience of one who witnesses and only expounds the essential qualities of love." – Isay Villena

"It is an emotional attachment to someone that intertwines with your soul. I think there are different types of love; the sweetest love I have ever known is that of my children. It's pure, unconditional, and true! It makes my heart race when I worry, physically hurts when I am scared for them. I put them before myself because their joy makes me happy." – Kelly Walk Hines

"It is selflessness. Instead of taking offense to something, it sees beyond the offense and to the pain of the person being offensive. It sees beyond anger jealousy or hate and responds with love instead because it seems that's what's missing. Sadly, we make the mistake of seeking love, not knowing the answer to what we seek is in the act of doing just that, loving someone else, and by becoming what we seek we attract it. It's the water to any fire and the hope for any despair." – Renee Browne

"Love is not 'like.' Love is not 'appreciate.' Love is not 'enjoy.' Love is not hugs, words, tears, smiles, or intimacy. Love is not shared memories and moments. Love is not human connection. Love is none of these. Love is ALL of these and more. Love can't be sold, bottled or packaged. Love is partly emotion, and partly the brain, the heart, and the soul—a potent combination. Love is reserved for people. The best dozen moments in your life, when you felt whole, bathed in the warmth of love, was probably due to human interaction. You may have later felt that same love again in the recollection of that epiphany. It is the deepest connection people can share. Guarding another's very being as you would your own. Allowing them to express themselves, and accept it, to know that they afford you the same graciousness and intimacy. Still, these descriptions all fall short of defining love. We know it once we experience it, yet we can't define it. Love is without explanation." – Jim Molinelli

WOW! I am just in awe and truly moved by these definitions. They are all beautiful and profound. You can tell how someone perceives love based on his or her experience, understanding, and belief. I believe their generosity to give love has positively and abundantly impacted their respective environments and communities.

But what if my question was to define self-love? The answers could be different. Defining self-love can be uncomfortable to some who may believe that love is selfless, and the thought of loving oneself might seem selfish, conceited, or narcissistic.

Some of us are so generous in giving love to others that we sometimes neglect loving ourselves. Some prefer to love others more because doing so makes them feel happy, it gives them a sense of purpose, and they expect their love to be reciprocated. Some have no choice because it scares them to be alone. But what will it be like when those loved ones leave us? Will we feel the same satisfaction and happiness? Who will take care and love us if we are already alone? Will we wait and look for someone until we feel complete, happy, satisfied, and loved again? Some may have answered, "God."

Where does God dwell? How do we experience love from the Infinite Source, isn't it through each one of us? The love from the Divine Source flows within everyone but not everyone knows of it, and not everyone believes it.

Our current relationships have so much fear involved. One sacrifices his needs, wants, and freedom to be his real self just to please the other. Almost everyone depends on each other to feel loved. Yes, relationships are important enough that we can experience our true essence and love. However, almost all relationships have higher expectations, as the belief is that one is incomplete without the love of the other. If one gives, then one must get something in return. The "I love you" becomes "I trade you."

Some cling to a relationship to feel safe and protected, and when relationships end, almost everyone succumbs to blaming and self-loathing. How can I say this? I had an experience that helped me realize this. Why is this occurring? We have based love on lack, conditions, and sources outside of us. We have forgotten that love is inside us, our true nature. **LOVE IS US.**

We have forgotten our authentic selves, and so we are in a continuous search for it in different places, situations, and people, believing that we are imperfect and incomplete beings. Therefore, an endless cycle takes place. The current condition of humanity is not in harmony and alignment with our true nature. This true nature has not been **fully** grasped yet by the majority. We have not fully accepted and believed it because everyone operates on a different level of awareness. **WE ARE LOVE** itself, with or without someone, as we are one with, and the physical extension of, the Source.

So how do we come back to love and understand and believe that we are it? By moment-to-moment

introspection and self-awareness. It is **time to look within us, understand why, change and grow** the way we see, label, and believe who and what we **truly** are. It is time to wake up and learn to love yourself!

REFLECTION:

How do you define love based on your life experiences?

What have you realized about love?

What lessons and wisdom did it teach you?

How do you connect yourself with love?

Do you see yourself as a source of love and love itself?

Why or why not?

CHAPTER THREE

THE JOURNEYS TO SELF-LOVE

Just like any relationship, when you meet someone whom you are interested in, you start with getting to know the other person. You excitedly try to find out his or her family background, status, and interests. Well, it's the same thing with having a relationship with yourself. This is how I started a loving relationship with myself. You start by knowing yourself further.

When I came across the question, "Who are you?" from one of the inspirational books I have read, and "Who were you before the world told you who you should be?" from one question circulating on the Internet I found years ago, I felt lost and confused. I did not have a clue how to answer these questions further apart from my usual and limited answers. I have never pondered so much on these questions before.

I was also asked the same question in a job interview and I remembered that I paused and wondered what the "right" answer was. I'd start with my name, my previous job experiences, education, and achievements, and if I want to go deeper or sound religious, I'd say I am a child of God without understanding the profundity of it.

It came to a point that my answers had no more depth for me and made little sense. That simple question seemed to be the hardest question I've thought of. I started a quest about the "self" so I could put this pondering to rest. I immersed myself in endless reading, searching, meditation, understanding spirituality, attending webinars on conscious living, watching videos of spiritual gurus, philosophers, life coaches, and listening to their teachings. I **asked** and **opened myself to receive** wisdom from whatever resource I could find, and it's evident even up to this day.

I went through different journeys that led me to love myself. These journeys benefited me in having a relationship with myself. I believe that you would, too. All these journeys became possible because of the **desire to know myself** and my **commitment** to that desire. Every journey started with an **open heart and mind** that led to its **rewiring** and **renewal**.

Every experience is unique and has a different revelation to every individual and every revelation has a different interpretation. Every person's journey to self-love is inimitable. May these journeys of mine inspire you.

THE JOURNEY OF SELF-DISCOVERY/INTROSPECTION

Since I could not answer the question, "Who am I?" I changed the question to "Who am I not?" This question had eliminated so many labels I identified myself with for as long as I could remember. It helped me distinguish my strengths, weaknesses, and passions.

I went to search for the word "self" in the dictionary before I ventured further. Among the several definitions of the word self, I resonated with the definition I found in the Cambridge Dictionary, which defined self as: "the set of someone's characteristics, such as personality and ability, that are **not physical** and make that person different from other people."

I used to think the self was more of my physical body, my skin, bones, and muscles. My personality, character, soul, and spirit were just add-ons. I was clueless as to why I classified them as such. I wasn't really into myself, meaning, I didn't know much about me and was not interested to know more.

In my quest to understand and know myself further, I came to realize that the real me is not one of the identities and images I've formed, conceptualized, and believed derived from the collection of thoughts I had about myself.

These identities are my name, nationality, gender, appearance, achievements, acquisitions, job, beliefs, background, and the role I play in society.

To be more specific, I am not my branded purses, expensive clothes, watches, jewelry, money in the bank, the house I live in, the nice car I drive, travels I've embarked on, educational degrees, job titles, and awards I have gained and achieved. These specifics were more to serve the physicality and for the egoistic identification that is based on form and none of the real me. I got stuck and attached to these labels, and perhaps you might have, too. I do not remember learning about consciousness or spiritual awareness anywhere, not even in school.

My way of living, thinking, making decisions, reasoning, and most of all, loving myself were all based on what I've done and gained that led and caused me to be hard on myself, especially in times of failure. I had the mentality of keeping up with the standards of society just to feel that I matter and I belong. I let the influences of other people and their beliefs affect me instead of living "my" life on my truth. It is enervating and futile.

I have been enraptured by this self-discovery journey. It caused me countless hours of searching, studying, and observing myself moment-to-moment. I sort of went through a reclusive phase where I detached myself from the outside world and looked in my inner world more.

I realized that a self-discovery journey is about **remembering** and **returning** to my **real self** that has **never** been **lost**. I was only **distracted** and have **forgotten** who I truly am. I am still remembering, learning, and experiencing more about me every moment of every single day, as a matter of fact. I would like to believe that humans are gods and goddesses just having temporary amnesia or under the influence of something else. You do not have to agree or disagree. Find out as you continue to read and through your own introspection.

In summary, these were my realizations that made perfect sense to remember the **real** me and perchance these could make sense to you, too:

1. That we are **SPIRITUAL BEINGS/CONSCIOUSNESS/ AWARENESS/SOULS/GODS AND GODDESSES/POWERFUL AND ETERNAL LOVING BEINGS**

Based on the different Bible scripture versions, I was reminded of these:

- *Proverbs 8:22-23 (NIV)*

  The Lord possessed me at the beginning of his work, the first of his acts of old. Ages ago I was set up, at the first, before the beginning of the earth.

- *John 17:16 (KJV)*

  They are not of the world, even as I am not of the world.

- *Genesis 1:27 (GNT)*

  So God created human beings, making them to be like himself. He created them male and female.

- *John 10:34 (ESV)*

  Jesus replied, "Is it not written in your Law: 'I have said you are gods'?"

- *Psalm 82:6 (NIV)*

  I said, "You are 'gods'; you are all sons of the Most High."

And inspired by the combined teachings of some spiritual gurus and inspirational teachers, philosophers, and authors I have interpreted theirs as:

- We came from the **non-physical realm** before we became physical human beings. We came from **nothingness; formlessness**, the **same energy source with the Divine**, and we are **pure consciousness**.

- We have God's DNA, making us the children of God, created in His/Her/Its own image and likeness. This means we are **gods and goddesses,** too. I am referring to the **capability** of humans **to love unconditionally** just like the masters who embodied love and walked this earth like Jesus Christ and Buddha.

- We were **individuated by the Divine Source** to **experience** humanity in the physical world, which led to the creation of the Universe so that the Infinite Creator/Divine Source/God would experience His/Her/Its Divine Self not only conceptually but also experientially through us.

- We are all **spiritual beings** having a human experience. There is no need for us to try hard to be spiritual as this is our nature. I understand that being spiritual is the knowing and being in touch with our divine self, our inner being, our higher self and our soul. It is looking within ourselves and understanding the truth inside of us.

- Us being the **consciousness awareness**, we are therefore the **observer** and **experiencer** of our thoughts and emotions. We are the **being** and the **knowing**—a **loving awareness**.

WHOA! These answered all questions about me as well as how one can exist in the physical world even if our true nature is non-physical.

How can we balance this? By being fully **conscious, aware, centered**, and **present** of what is—every event, activity, emotion, thought, experience, and life that is unfolding in front of you without being attached, affected, and reactive.

You and I are conscious because we are alive, feeling our body and our surroundings. It's about our experiences. We are aware because we recognize this consciousness and know that we exist. We are centered and present in the seat of the self when we remain observers and witnesses of the events without causing us to react. It is letting the present moment unfold without the need to label, judge, control, manipulate, and resist but just surrender in the present moment. We have become used to reacting and, in so doing, we have forgotten to just be . . . being . . . human being and not a human doing.

Here are simple ways to understand consciousness awareness:

Imagine you're about to watch your favorite show. Before it starts, you are aware of your surroundings such as your living room, your couch, and the other person seated next to you. Once it starts and progresses, you find your consciousness so absorbed in the show that you feel all the emotions. Eventually, you forget your surroundings and that other person in the room, as if the show was your reality. As soon as the show ends, you realize your surroundings again and you're back to your original state of consciousness. You realize again you were only the observer (the surroundings, the one watching TV, the other person in the room, the show being watched, the shift in consciousness, and the sensations felt).

Observe yourself when you sit quietly for a minute or two. Initially, you're aware that you are seated, still, and quiet. Observe how your consciousness suddenly focuses on one thought, the object of your consciousness, and you eventually feel the sensations brought by that chosen thought that grabbed your attention. You forgot about that original state of consciousness you were in, just sitting quietly on the couch.

You noticed the change in your consciousness. That's your awareness. And that's who you really are—the free consciousness who noticed and realized all these. You are not of your thoughts and emotions but just the observer, the one who witnesses all the unfolding events in front of you.

Do you remember a time when you were engaged in a conversation with another person and you suddenly realized that you were no longer listening and focused on what the other person was talking about? You found your consciousness wandering, lost in some thoughts your mind was showing you. Then you had to go back to your original state of consciousness and apologize and ask the other person to repeat the topic. You are the observer of the change in consciousness, conversation, and people in conversation.

What about the expression "I was not myself" when I did or said hurtful things to someone out of anger? There was a realization that took place after the release of the emotion because you went back to your original state of consciousness, which is love. You're the awareness of the incident and the shift of consciousness that took place.

As beings of consciousness and awareness, nothing hurts, binds, and affects you, as you are only the observer and experiencer of how the present moment unfolds. Remember the power I mentioned during my lowest times that caused me to feel whole despite circumstances? That's the same consciousness awareness I am talking about here. It's indestructible. It's stillness and calmness in the storm.

Nothing can destroy you. You are beyond your physical body that is subject to limitations. You only experience limitations and sensations when your consciousness gets consumed in your thoughts and emotions. The moment you allow yourself to entertain a thought, it affects you in many aspects of your life. I realize that as long as I identify myself with the physical body, I continue to suffer. Remember, you and I belong to the same consciousness of the Divine, which is about peace, joy, and love. So when you ponder these, everything here in the physical world is not our reality but just an illusion, a dream. We are limitless and boundless. Everything is happening and being shown and identified only by the mind that is the creator of thoughts.

Each moment and experience gives each one of us a **choice** whether to be affected by it or not. Can you imagine if all of us knew that we are the awareness? We would stop being personal and sensitive about things, people, and situations. We can truly have peaceful and joyful lives.

2. That we were created **COMPLETE** and **PERFECT** by the Infinite and Perfect Creator.

We were made through the image and likeness of the Infinite Creator. We should never look at ourselves as imperfect and incomplete. How can we consider ourselves imperfect when the One who created us is perfect and complete? We were not made a percentage less or more.

There have been so many teachings and influences about how flawed and bad we are, and that we are not worthy of God's love. Perhaps this is something that humanity has to look into and consider changing the perception and narrative about it. No longer should we need someone and something to validate, tell, and make us feel whole and complete, as we already are! We are enough! We are all created complete and perfect just as we are! We are here to discover and remember and experience our greatness from our mistakes.

3. That we are **VIBRATIONAL CREATIVE BEINGS**—we are not just our physical bodies but also more.

I am not a scientist but understand everything is in motion and everything is energy is through the laws of the Universe: Law of Vibration and Law of Attraction.

Our consciousness is a mixture of thoughts and emotions. Thoughts are energies and so are emotions. We are in an environment where everything vibrates. Our human body, for example, has massive amounts of energy locked up in molecules, composed of several atoms in high-speed vibration. We can compare the Universe to a field of consciousness—a magnetic field of energies and vibrations. If you dig deeper, this Universe is us. We are energy beings, emitting frequencies through our chosen thoughts and emotions as the focus of our attention. **Whatever we think and believe, we become**, and whatever we **feel** or vibrate tells us if we are in alignment with the Source energy and our higher self, responding to the Law of Attraction creating our reality. This law is the primal law of the Universe. It is mirroring back to us whatever energy or vibration we give out and **works effectively when we are in the same vibration of whatever we desire.** Therefore, we are the deliberate creators of our reality and a co-creator of the Infinite One.

The simplest example of how this Law of Attraction and Law of Vibration works is: If you desire wealth, then you have to be in the same vibration of feeling, acting, and living as if you are already wealthy without a doubt. Focus on how the wealthy people feel. The Universe then responds to the same vibration you are emitting. Like energy attracts like energy.

I have a lot of manifestation experiences through the power of our thoughts such as finding a parking spot right away during busy hours. When driving in a public parking lot, I would picture in my mind, with feelings of excitement and gratitude that a parking spot is already waiting for me even before I arrive in the parking area. And voila, it usually happens without waiting. How did it happen? The thoughts and emotions are all aligned and in harmony, vibrating in one frequency so the Universe has no other way but to bring it to fruition. The biggest factor here is the **belief** that everything will happen. You cannot declare or say positive words but feel negative. Nothing manifests if there's no belief that it will. The Universe listens to how you **feel**.

Another manifestation experience is my healing from Aplastic Anemia. Again, I visualized myself healthy, with feelings of happiness, gratitude, and faith. In less than four years, doctors cleared me, and we didn't even need to go through the bone marrow transplant they initially proposed. From then onward, I've been in excellent health attested to by the positive results of my annual physical exams. Just so you know, you are unconsciously doing this every single day. You are thinking of and consumed by thoughts every moment. You can tell the quality of your thoughts by what you are attracting in your life now. The good thing is that you, as the master observer of your thoughts, have a choice where to focus your attention.

4. That we are **NOT OF OUR EGOS** is the illusory image we have created of ourselves through and from our mind.

Ego does **NOT** operate on love but on fear, superiority, survival, and separation. Some said it is bad and we should eradicate it, but as I navigate this spiritual awakening, I only see this ego as a tool to warn me in this world of polarity. It warns me whether I am operating and intending my life based on form or from the spiritual part of me. Perhaps we can be **fully aware and present** of the true self instead of eradicating the ego. I only consider it as a vice if it has consumed and blinded me, and I become attached to it. But I believe that we are all bound to wake up, realize, and remember who we truly are as nothing stays permanent. Every moment of every day we are creating anew ourselves, our life story, and life experience.

5. That we are **ONE WITH ALL, THE UNIVERSE, GOD, EARTH, PEOPLE, AND OTHER SENTIENT BEINGS** as

everything came from the same consciousness, Infinite Source, the Divine Source, God. And so, whatever we do to ourselves affects all of humanity. Notice our world lately? The earth as it is can survive without us. It has been in harmonious existence with other sentient beings before we came along. Our contributions to the environment, community, and society have resulted in the state we are in. It is up to us to decide how we will maintain its original state and this oneness.

I was awash with awe and joy upon realizing, learning, and remembering all these. I keep discovering myself from every moment, the choices and decisions I make, emotions I feel and manage, relationships I have, the circle of people I surround myself with and people I meet, books I read, music I listen to, places I go, and most of all, how I give and receive love.

We are more than what we appear to be on the surface. What awesome beings we are! If we all accept, believe, and live as loving awareness, our world will change to what we prefer it to be. If we realize who we are, there will be no wars, competition, pain, and suffering.

We can just share in the abundance, unity, peace, harmony, and love for each other instead. Despite each of us going through different paths to enlightenment, and each of us having different points of views about ourselves and the world according to our own level of awareness, I believe there is a shift of consciousness happening, a new hope is being felt despite current dictation of events, a new earth is rising, we are evolving. We are weary of the egoistic sense of self; we are going back to the Divine

Source, going back to our true nature, our original state—the state of oneness—Love.

REFLECTION ON SELF-DISCOVERY:

Who are you?

Who are you not?

What do you know about yourself?

What do you identify yourself with? How does labeling your identity serve you?

How did you find out more about you?

What has been revealed in your self-discovery/introspection journey so far?

THE JOURNEY OF SELF-ACCEPTANCE

It can be difficult to accept oneself, especially when lost in life's experiences and influenced by different programming and beliefs that we created. These experiences and brainwashing resulted in seeing and treating myself as separate from God, a flawed human being and eternally in need of salvation. I have lived in fear, guilt, and shame for every mistake. I felt I couldn't do anything right in my life. I saw the world as a lonely, judgmental place. I've been hard on myself and became doubtful of my capabilities and talents. It was a sad experience, and I felt alone, hungry for approval, and felt unworthy of being loved by anyone, especially the Infinite Creator.

I experienced so much bickering in my family while I was growing up. I witnessed my mother's devastation when my father's business faced bankruptcy, and it affected their relationship and the entire family. It took a toll on everyone. We lived in the mentality of lack and fear. There was too much tension at home. We became anxious and stressed to the point we could no longer stand each other. My parents have infused in our minds that we need to have something—be it recognition, wealth, education—to be valued and be accepted by society, otherwise we are "nothing"—a nobody. This foundation taught me to base my worth on what society thinks of me, through the material things I have, my financial stability, and my accomplishments. I went through a stage of plenty and a stage of lack. I realized that I was tough on myself especially in the stage of lack. I felt empty, insecure, had low self-esteem, worried about what other people would say about me, blamed myself for the result of what only I can achieve, and I was fearful of my future.

I have learned to accept myself by doing the following:

I changed my perception and narrative about God and myself. I started my self-acceptance by acknowledging my true nature, which is the same consciousness of the Divine Source and my partnership with God. Because of my Near-Death-Experience (NDE), I neither see a God who is judgmental and vengeful nor a God who would punish my every mistake. I changed the way I believed in and saw God. I changed the narrative that I was exposed to since I was a kid. I see and experience God with more of a loving awareness and as one with me. God is the Source of all love, the Infinite Perfect Creator who created everything perfectly, including you and me. I no longer see myself as a physical being but beyond it, a beautiful being and soul in union with the Divine Source, **worthy** of all love. I now see myself with greater meaning and depth—a co-creator of the Infinite Creator. I realized that I am always whole, even without material things, because I am not these things.

I looked at myself with compassion. I stopped judging myself. I realized that being judgmental is coming from a place of having a fixed mindset and lack. This is a about a lack of understanding. I noticed that when I'm not judging, I'm more open to understanding and learning from my experience. Because of this, I understood my feelings, emotions, actions, and myself more. I treated myself with more patience and kindness.

I became more observant of myself. I noted the things I can and cannot accept about myself. On the things I can't accept, I'll try to find out why they became unacceptable in the first place and turn them into positives. These can vary from my physical appearance, personality, how I talk, how I act, how I operate, and how I live my life. When I **shifted** my consciousness to be more accepting of myself, I received more appreciation and admiration from people. When I accepted myself, people accepted me, too. Why? I sent out positive energy, which attracted like energy, then mirrored back at me. Remember, thoughts are energy.

I accepted myself the way I am. I now know that I am loved and not judged by God. And so I accept my mistakes and imperfections. No longer do I make a big deal about them like I used to. I accept my physical appearance as is, whether I lose or gain weight, or when I discover gray hair or new wrinkles. I became more grateful for how my body marvelously and miraculously operates and functions every single day. I have also learned to accept my unique personality as I no longer depend on someone's approval of me, as I know that our Infinite Perfect Creator has approved of me from the moment I was born. Pleasing people and apologizing for being my authentic self is no longer needed. I'm the only person who understands and knows why I have my personality. I accept, welcome, and receive compliments from other people with gladness, and I own and embrace them with confidence. I also understand that negative reactions from other people are none of my concern as those reactions are the awareness of themselves coming from the beliefs they have experienced.

I stopped comparing myself to other people. I have realized that the reason we compare ourselves with one another is that we come from a mindset of lack and separation. One might find and make sense of his worth from what others have. And so, I stopped comparing myself with others as it made me feel less and bad about myself. I have learned how to stop being influenced by the ego-driven society where everyone is in competition on who has more. When I understood how the ego operates and survives—in fear and always hungry for attention—I became more focused and aware of the **"deeper I"** or the **real me**, which has no requirements and is liberating. This is the living I find more meaningful. I **fixed my thinking,** viewing people as my inspiration rather than my competition.

I learned to be content with what I can and cannot do, and where I am now. I now know that I am doing just fine, and I know that I am enough. I accept myself whether I've achieved too little, just enough, or too much. It is well with my soul. I rest on the knowledge that an Infinite Perfect Creator created me perfectly and wonderfully. I accept the unconditional love of the Infinite Source.

Self-acceptance is **allowing** yourself to just be in the moment of now. It is surrender instead of resistance. It starts with a renewal of your mindset on how you perceive yourself, followed by the openness of your heart to appreciation and gratitude. It is **deciding** that you will agree and with contentment on how you look and operate your life the way you prefer it to be without guilt, doubts, and questions. It is **honoring** your experience and being at **peace** with it.

By focusing more on your positives, you will find more. When you love your negatives, they turn into your positives, too. One should no longer desire approval and acceptance from others as you have already been approved the moment you existed in this world. There is too much love from the Universe to feel disapproval of yourself. Embrace your weirdness. Enjoy being the unique you!

REFLECTION ON SELF-ACCEPTANCE:

How do you see yourself?

What do you resist the most about yourself?

Do you accept yourself as you are? If not, what are the unacceptable parts, attitudes, and behavior of you that you need to work on?

How did they become unacceptable?

How did you accept yourself? What are the steps you have done to accept yourself?

THE JOURNEY OF SELF-FORGIVENESS AND SELF-UNDERSTANDING

Forgiving myself means remembering, believing, and accepting my true nature of peace, joy, and love. Since there's an awareness that I am the **awareness**, I changed my perception about people. It became easy for me to forgive other people, even my parents, for all the physical and verbal abuses I experienced from them. I looked through and understood them, and that led me to see them as beautiful souls, just like every other being on this earth. I looked through them the way God looked through me: with love.

I used the following steps to help me process forgiveness to myself:

I looked through me. I learned to see my inner being and higher self by being conscious and aware of it. I focused more on the beauty and love that's in me.

I stopped the judgment. I realized that I am my number one enemy, critic, and judge and that these judgments come from the thoughts I continuously entertain in my mind, not from other sources. I replaced judgment with appreciation. I faced them with the confidence that I am simply loved and not judged by our unconditionally loving God.

I stopped the blame. I replaced the blame approach with appreciation, compassion, and gentleness toward myself, whether or not I have accomplished a goal. I became more patient with myself. I don't give up on me now. I no longer feel frustrated at myself.

I freed myself. I released myself from any negative emotional bondage, especially from the past. I have learned that I am the creator of my reality and so the past no longer controls me. I made peace with it and have moved on. I can let go now. I choose to be happy.

I live in the now. I realized that the present moment has demands only when I choose thoughts that do not serve me and when I add negative stories to the stillness of the now. I also learned that all the activities, events, and my plans for the future are happening and will happen in the moment of now. Having this clarity of the present moment, I allow myself to just be with and revel in it.

Forgiveness is about love. When you grasp the word for-give, it is really about giving. Giving yourself and other people love and giving yourself the freedom to live happily without restrictions and conditions. I also learned that when understanding is present, forgiveness is no longer needed, as an act was already deemed acceptable even before the need to forgive arises. One has already understood the reasons behind every being's actions and decided in his heart that forgiveness is no longer needed. Freedom is sweet and a celebration for the soul.

REFLECTION ON SELF-FORGIVENESS:

Have you forgiven yourself? If not, what is stopping you?

How did you set yourself free?

What were the steps you took to forgive yourself?

What changes have you noticed in your life after you forgave yourself?

THE JOURNEY OF SELF-HEALING/SELF-CARE

Healing is all about your well-being and living your life to the fullest. It is about your happiness, satisfaction, and being in touch with your spirituality while in this physical body. As with everything, the right mindset, commitment, and openness to learn, accept, and receive changes are necessary. It involves self-care and nurturing, which takes place in various ways for every individual. I realized that to live a blissful life, I should be in **alignment** with the consciousness of the Divine Source. This is about the loving awareness, like how the masters who walked on this earth have lived and inspired us. For continuous healing, I focused on maintaining awareness, working on my mind, body, and spirit.

Mind

Loving yourself is not a challenge as the challenge is only in your mind. The only thing that comes between you and healing is your mind. The mind is like a machine that creates thoughts. Thoughts are energies. They come and go. They are the noises in your mind you can't silence most of the time. You cannot control nor remove thoughts. You as the awareness are the stillness that is immovable. The majority of these noises or thoughts are from the past you haven't handled or dealt with. Some are just worries and anxieties for things that haven't happened yet. Some are the beliefs of the collective consciousness that affect you. As a result, they're stored and stuck inside you, troubling you for several years. A single thought, be it positive or negative, when entertained consistently becomes a belief, which then forms a behavior and affects your perception of yourself, people, and situations. It shapes your life if you are not careful. The good thing is that you can do something about it. You have choices on how to handle it. The goal here is for you to live your best by having a peaceful, quiet, and open mind, not subjected to any beliefs or labeling.

- It is important to be **mindful** at all times by being the **boss** of your mind. It requires you to be **conscious** of your thought choices and **aware** of your experience of the present moment and enjoying that experience. Mindfulness prompts you to decide how to use your mind, constructively or destructively.

- It is also imperative to know that you are the consciousness who is the **observer** and **chooser** of your thoughts. You are **not** your mind or your thoughts. There will always be thoughts of negative and positive as we live in a world of contrast. When I realized thoughts are energies that can manifest through constant attention, I became **conscious** of my thought pattern.

- You have the **power to release** and **let thoughts slip by, especially those that do not serve you.** Feed your mind by choosing good thoughts.

- When consumed by a negative thought, **you can deal with it by changing it right away without being reactive or needing to judge it. Remain in awareness.** Meditation, napping, and deep breathing exercises help your **focus** and **clarity** and that leads to a peaceful mind. When focus and clarity are present, your life becomes more organized.

- If you can't be aware of your thoughts, **pay attention to how you feel.** I discovered that my sadness, worries, anger, emotions, and even illnesses originated from the **quality** of thought I allowed myself to think about and be affected by. These emotions are the manifestation of the repetitive thoughts that I had from the past that appeared in the present and had me worried about the future.

Body

This is all about your wellness. It requires commitment and discipline. The goal here is to keep you healthy, and so the mindset should be in alignment with this. You can treat it as your only clothing to wear. Wherever you go, you are always with your one and only earth suit and so you might as well take care in this lifetime. Every individual is different in treating and taking care of the body and the daily workout routine and goals. You can find something that suits your needs. Your body is the vessel where the energy flows and the manifestation and physical extension of the Divine Source to experience humanity. You can maintain it not only through exercise and the quality of food and drink you take in but also by:

- Being mindful to what you expose yourself to. Be **responsible** for the **energy** that you bring into your life. Surround yourself with more positive and happy influences from media, places, and most especially from people.

- Changing your **self-talk** from negative and judgmental to **encouraging, uplifting, and positive** conversations. Always talk to yourself lovingly.

- Continuously **creating** and **finding inspiration** in everything. I find writing to be therapeutic. It is my expression of creativity. It is my contribution to the betterment of humanity and my connection with people. You can find and do something you are passionate about, something fun, easy, and that makes you **happy.** We can never run out of things to do as we are in a constant process of creation and evolution.

- **Humor** is an excellent source for good health as it opens your heart to the positive flow of energy affecting your body as opposed to hatred, anger, and sadness. Laugh at yourself, your silliness, and mistakes. Life is to be enjoyed. Create the environment you would like to be in as everything springs forth from you starting from your conscious choice of thoughts and from the knowledge that you are the loving awareness.

Spirit

It is our true nature. It is about peace, joy, and love. The goal here is to be more in touch with your spiritual, non-physical nature. I believe that we have to be in alignment with it by living in full **awareness**.

- Expose and immerse yourself with the works of the different spiritual authors, gurus, and philosophers on a regular basis. It helps you further discover and remember your inner being/higher self. You have a choice to apply the wisdom from their teachings that **only serve and work** for you. Their teachings helped me activate the inner guidance that each one of us has. I consider them as my support system apart from my family and a few friends. You can check the works of the following people: Ramana Maharshi, Lao Tzu, J. Krishnamurti, John Murphy, Alan Watts, Neville Goddard, Dr. Wayne Dyer, Ram Dass, Thich Nhat Hanh, Robert Spira, Eckhart Tolle, Deepak Chopra, Abraham Hicks, Bob Proctor, Barbara Hubbard, Neale Donald Walsch, Joel Osteen, Michael Singer,

Marianne Williamson, and many more. There are many reflections on the life of Jesus Christ and Buddha, too.

- **Meditate**. Give yourself some **quiet time** and observe. Silence reveals a lot of inspiration, wisdom, and guidance. Listen to your soul. It's always talking to you. Always go back to the center and seat of your Soul/Self by being **still** and enjoying the **present** moment.

- **Prayers of appreciation** and **affirmations** that are focused on wellness, prosperity, and other specific desires or goals you'd like to achieve are excellent suggestions to your subconscious. It's through repetition or the habitual thinking of a specific thought/idea that the subconscious mind works. Once an idea sinks in, the subconscious mind will bring it to manifestation. You can check these links:

  https://en.wikipedia.org/wiki/Habit

  https://youtu.be/3DwUunAN0Vs

  https://www.amazon.com/Power-Your-Subconscious-Mind/dp/160459201X

  https://www.louisehay.com/101-best-louise-hay-positive-affirmations/

- You can deal with emotions by **allowing** yourself to experience and understand them from a **seeker** mindset rather than a victim mindset. Then you can ask yourself these questions: **Why**

am I feeling this way? What is this experience teaching me? These questions help you in your spiritual growth. Learn something new about yourself and move on rather than being stuck and being a victim, drowning in drama and feeling hopeless. You are never a victim; only your thoughts say you are. It is normal to cry and feel pain, but the goal is to free yourself from unnecessary energy you expose yourself to.

- You can **free** yourself from **too much expectation** from other people. You can continue to be your own friend, supporter, encourager, inspirer, empowerer, motivator, and lover as the expectation from other resources can cause heartaches and disappointments if not met. Everyone sees the world according to his or her own lens, perception, and level of awareness. Not all will be ready for you. I am not proposing nor referring to isolation. I am letting you know the power inside you.

- You can **acknowledge, learn, and appreciate** the disparity of events, as you know these events are the manifestations of the focus of your attention and the thoughts of the collective. There is always inspiration from everything.

- You can live a life of **non-resistance** and more of **acceptance and faith in the Universe** as everything you experience works for your benefit and expansion. Look for its meaning and purpose instead of the disadvantages. Learn to

let go of the things that do not serve you, such as negative reactions from people and society's behaviors, as these are the things beyond your control. However, there are matters worth elevating to raise more awareness especially when there is imminent harm.

- You can ask yourself these questions daily for guidance in all your activities: **Why am I here? Who am I? What is my intention? What is it I have that I'm not aware of? What is the Universe trying to show and tell me that I may not see nor hear?** If I have healed and still continue to heal, you can, too.

REFLECTION ON SELF-HEALING:

How do you take care of yourself?

How do you heal?

What steps have you taken to achieve healing?

Have you committed to healing yourself?

CHAPTER FOUR

UNDERSTANDING SELF-LOVE

There is no doubt or question that each one of us can generously love one another, but love without forgetting ourselves, too. How can you fill someone's cup if your cup is already empty? How can you help others when you yourself need help? A blind man cannot lead another blind man. Where will they go? What can be accomplished?

Based on the word itself, one can say self-love is about loving oneself. But what does self-love mean? It seems much easier to define how to love other people than it is to love oneself. How is it so? Perhaps some of you might relate to the following reasons it is difficult to love oneself:

- The fear of losing other people, your partners, families, and friends, as the focus of attention is on yourself

- The fear of being misinterpreted by others because of influences/beliefs/sayings of the collective that it is selfish to love yourself before others

- The fear of rejection by other people for having a different opinion from the norm
- The fear of being alone
- The fear of being different and weird
- The belief of being unworthy because of perceived imperfections

And so, because of these reasons we tend to:

- Depend on people's approval
- Expect more from others to help fill the void
- Ruin relationships
- Have low self-esteem/confidence
- Self-loathe
- Self-reject
- Deny one's needs
- Lose focus of our dreams
- Lose our identity
- Lose our uniqueness
- Be dissatisfied

- Be envious and jealous of others
- Live in despair
- Live in anxiety

After the journeys I have taken, I understood myself further, learned the true essence of the self, and loved myself freely without restrictions. These definitions are geared toward self-awareness.

Based on my experience and realization, I share and define Self-Love in these ways:

1. **It is the knowing of yourself**. You remember yourself on a deeper level. You see yourself not only physically but also spiritually and shift your attention to the inner self. You make yourself the center of your attention, which has nothing to do with conceit, narcissism, selfishness, neglect, or and even hating people. Start by showing interest in further understanding and building a relationship with yourself. You can only know and understand others when you fully know and understand yourself. To know oneself is equivalent to loving you. A well-loved self can supply an abundance of love for all.

2. **It is distinguishing your nature.** You recognize that you are the loving awareness who came from pure consciousness. You focus through you rather than at you. You are love itself.

3. **It is the awakening of the self**. You recognize yourself as beyond a physical human being but

more of a spiritual being having the human experience. You realize that you are the physical extension of the Source Energy, and co-creator of the Infinite Creator. You are a vessel through which the Divine Source flows, an indestructible spirit.

4. **It is the alignment with the Divine Source and with your true self**. This is the realization that you are the expression of love itself. It is you, as love, who loves.

5. **It is the recognition that you are complete**. You are confident. You accept and believe that an Infinite and Perfect Creator made you complete and perfect. You are an extraordinary being. Nothing is lacking nor is more about you. You are enough.

6. **It is the awareness and recognition of your power within**. You see yourself in a whole new perspective. You consider yourself beyond how you perceived yourself from the past. You realize that you are boundless and limitless. You believe everything is possible. You discover your strengths, gifts, and your full potential as a being of this planet and use them consciously and confidently. You have the power to change your life by renewing your mindset.

7. **It is the learning to interpret the language of your intuitive heart**. You acknowledge, honor, and become more sensitive and dependent on your intuition and emotions as guidance. Your heart is not just an organ in your body but the center of

your energies. It is where your energy flows. It creates vibrations and harmonies that only you can understand and perceive. You take notice of your environment through your intuition rather than your senses.

8. **It is the recognition of your truth.** You know exactly where you are and the premise you stand for where you can grow and discover more of your authentic self.

9. **It is freedom from influences, conditioning, programming, and beliefs**. Focus only on your own truth and beliefs. Free yourself from those who do not serve you and limit you from your growth and freedom. It is freedom from the egoistic self. It is rejoicing in the soul's knowledge about you.

10. **It is the knowing that your inner being sees and loves you**. You know that you're not judged but instead loved by your higher self, the soul, the God within you.

11. **It is being responsible and being a steward of your gifts**. You recognize that you are not just a physical body but more. You were born with abilities and wisdom you can use for your personal and everyone's well-being. You are an extraordinary being.

12. **It is the strength and ability to forgive and accept yourself for who and what you are**. You release yourself from the bondage that stops you from living the life you so deserve—peaceful, joyful, and

full of love. You focus on healing and remembering your true beauty inside.

13. **It is the courage to move forward**. You embrace and enjoy the moment of now rather than remaining stuck in the past. You shift your consciousness to the present moment. You open yourself to more exciting changes and possibilities leading to a brighter future.

14. **It is the welcoming of blessings**. You see yourself worthy and deserving of love. You allow yourself not only to give love but also to openly and gladly receive it.

15. **It is not selfish**. You generously love yourself first so you experience it and give love to others based on love and not on need and expectation.

16. **It is living a life without resistance and conflict**. You trust the love of the Infinite Universe and the Divine Source that you allow things to happen as they are, consider them as blessings and acknowledge their timing. Everything works for your benefit, regardless of how it may seem. You look at challenges as your learning experiences, identifying what works and serves you. Everything happens for your advancement.

17. **It is creating a new you**. You start by making the unconscious conscious, dis-creating old belief patterns, welcoming, and replacing new ones. You focus on a new mindset, more positive and healing thoughts, a new life, and you train yourself to see

things from a new perspective. Let go of old paradigms that no longer serve you.

18. **It is loving yourself as you are, for who and what you are**. You allow yourself to just be. You embrace your uniqueness and weirdness. You are satisfied with how you look, how you speak, what you have, how you act, how you present yourself, how you live your life, and how you were made by our Infinite Creator.

19. **It is being at peace with your negatives**. You accept that it is all right to make mistakes, as these are bound to happen. You are a creative being, and these mistakes do not define you but are part of the creation process. You look away from the false flaws you see in yourself resulting in inferiority. You focus more on the perfection of how the Infinite Creator has created you, knowing you are consciousness and loving awareness.

20. **It is praising yourself**. You appreciate yourself every time for every little thing you do and accomplish and even if you do nothing. You are patient and considerate of yourself, and by doing this, you encourage yourself more.

21. **It is doing the things that make you happy**. You do things that bring out the best in you, excite you, bring you love, bring out the creativity and passion in you. You use your talents and you help and inspire people to do the same. You also delight in and enjoy your own company.

22. **It is honoring and living your own experience**. You live in your own truth, you believe and are confident in your own voice and choices. You no longer compare your life with the life of others as models on how you should live yours.

23. **It is validating your feelings**. You acknowledge and honor your feelings. You allow yourself to feel and experience your emotion instead of just ignoring it. You discover and learn from the experience and do not become consumed and victimized.

24. **It is focusing on feeling good**. You only pay attention to sources that give you peace, happiness, bliss, and joy.

25. **It is gratitude toward yourself**. You are grateful for your entirety, your nature, your existence in this Universe, your purpose, how your body operates and functions, and your ideas for expansion in your life that keeps on unfolding.

26. **It is saying NO**. You choose what works and serves your purpose. You select what is good and beneficial for your growth and expansion. You set up boundaries against any negativity to protect your energy.

27. **It is the acceptance of yourself according to your own definition instead of how others define you**. You value and acknowledge more of how you see yourself rather than how others see you.

28. **It is dis-empowering other people's disapproval of you**. You live in your own approval and not on the approval of others. You know who you are and believe that God has approved of you first. People will always have something negative to say about you. They are just holding you as the subject of their weaknesses or discontentment in themselves.

29. **It is the power to let go**. You withdraw from things, situations, and people that do not serve your purpose. You choose to be mindful of what and whom you surround and expose yourself with and stay in the seat of the centered Self, which is the loving awareness. You let go of guilt, blame, and shame you have carried inside you and make peace with yourself.

30. **It is choosing the right self-talk**. You no longer talk to yourself in fear. You remind and affirm yourself of your power, beauty, and oneness with the Divine Intelligence. You talk to yourself without criticism and judgment but kindly, positively, encouragingly and lovingly. You learn that through your repetitive self-talks of healing and love as examples, the subconscious mind will approve of it and ensure its fruition—a healthy, disease-free body and a lovely aura.

31. **It is being kind to your mind**. You choose thoughts that create more love and appreciation for yourself. You engage in meditation for focus and clarity. You observe your thought quality. You allow empowering and encouraging thoughts instead of

damaging ones. Free yourself from overthinking. Visualize only positive images.

32. **It is treating your body with care**. You take good care of yourself physically. You honor and respect your body through regular exercise and healthy eating and drinking. You become conscious of what you expose your body to. You give yourself time to relax and meditate.

33. **It is communing with nature**. You appreciate the beauty of nature and other sentient beings. You respect the earth and our environment. When you love and take care of yourself, you treat every being on the planet the same, realizing that you are all connected as one.

34. **It is seeing other people as you are**. You see yourself in others. You are one and interconnected with everyone. You understand, forgive, accept, and allow people to be themselves the same way you have understood, forgiven, accepted, and allowed yourself to be you. Build stronger relationships, achieve oneness, and establish harmony, peace, and unity with one another thus diminishing hatred.

35. **It is the cessation from being self-righteous**. You recognize everyone as your equals. All are special and a source of peace, joy, and love. You focus only on changing yourself, not fixing and changing others, as you can only encourage, motivate, inspire, and empower instead of impose and dictate.

36. **It has no expectation from other people**. You recognize, acknowledge, and respect that every individual's level of awareness and understanding differs from yours. You also acknowledge that you're made complete while expecting validation from others. Share in each other's completeness, achieving quality relationships with everyone.

I realize that I am the only one accountable for loving myself. I understand that self-love is not just about loving oneself but freeing oneself from the conflicts of this world, derived from the chosen thoughts based on ego, which is the only thing that keeps everyone from loving each other the right way. What I understood mostly is that self-love is the **experience and acknowledgement of my oneness and union with the Infinite Creator/Source/God**.

I can only encourage and motivate you to start and focus on knowing, appreciating, accepting, understanding, forgiving, and loving yourself for who you are and what you are at this very moment. Free yourself from the noises of your mind. Stillness, emptiness, and quietness have a lot of wisdom to share with you. Every single moment of every day you are with yourself, so you might as well have a love affair with yourself!

REFLECTION:

What is self-love to you?

How is your relationship with yourself?

What can you do to help you love yourself?

How do you love yourself?

CHAPTER FIVE
THE SELF-LOVE EFFECT

The Effects of Self-Love

You become a master observer and master of the self. Any occurrence in life doesn't easily affect you.

You become the embodiment of freedom from the beliefs of limitations and fear. You inspire people to practice introspection leading to emancipation.

You become resilient and fearless because of the knowledge, belief, and confidence that you are a co-creator of the Infinite One, the physical extension of the Divine Source.

You become peaceful and forgiving of others because of the assurance that you are loved and not judged by our Infinite Creator.

You become healthier as you are no longer controlled by your thoughts, especially those that cause stress and depression.

You become self-assured as you trust yourself more for becoming a being of power. You are no longer fearful of being alone. You feel loved and complete even by yourself.

You are more confident as you are no longer concerned and affected by other people's opinion of you.

You become open and welcoming, as energies of peace, joy, bliss, and love freely flow through you, inspiring and motivating people to be in these states.

You become more attractive with the way you present and carry yourself, and it draws people to your positive energy, inspiring them to love themselves, too.

You become the hope for others as you help them see challenges from a different perspective, strengthening and guiding them to see theirs as an opportunity for growth rather than a threat.

You become a bringer of light to those in the dark, giving them clarity and empowerment and helping them realize and ignite the light inside them.

You become compassionate and understanding as you see other people like you, achieving unity and oneness.

You have a purposeful life living a continuous exploration of yourself as the loving awareness and creative expansion of joy.

You are present-oriented.

You have more wisdom in parenting your emotions.

You have better relationships with people as you have established a better relationship with yourself.

You are in harmony and in alignment with the Infinite Source of love.

I love what I have become and love what I am becoming because of self-love. I will not tell you to love yourself NOW. I will not even ask you if not now when. I will only encourage you to at least start by knowing who you are. Let that inner well of wisdom inside you reveal itself. The true self has to be realized. Knowing your true essence and loving ourselves enables us to see it in each other.

Observe and understand your reactions, consciousness, and self in all situations. Learn and discover your greatness and power within as a SPIRITUAL being. Be in touch with your Divine self. Find your truth, live it, and grow in spirit and love. Create a world where love abounds and unity, peace, harmony, advancement, and ease are evident. We are just walking each other home, back to God.

Come back to your being of loving awareness.

Come back to God.

Come back to love.

REFLECTION:

What are the effects of self-love in your life?

Are there any changes you noticed in yourself?

How did you benefit from loving yourself?

SELF-LOVE

The greatest love
The most forgotten love
The taken-for-granted love
The taken-out-of-context love
The difficult-to-master love

In its incessant absence
Hatred rules the earth
Judgment is present
Separation in men is evident

In this world of polarity
One cannot exist without the other
If hatred can be given away
So can love

Come back to love, oh beautiful men
For so long you have lived in hate
No more blaming yourselves
Allow yourselves to love again
As your nature has always been love

Self-love
You forgive you for what you are
You accept you for who you are

You see you and in each and everyone
You unite with other souls
A love that is significant to men

By: Elsa Mendoza From the book:
Wake Up Humanity Poems About You and Me

REQUEST

If you have enjoyed my book, it would be greatly appreciated if you left a review so others can receive the same benefits you have. Your review will help me see what is and isn't working so I can better serve you and all my other readers even more.

ACKNOWLEDGEMENTS

I am eternally thankful to our Divine Intelligence for inspiring me to write this book.

To you, beautiful soul, reader, supporter, and believer of my works, I am in gratitude to you for purchasing my books. I am so inspired to write more.

To the people who took their time and effort to define love based on their respective experiences, I truly appreciate each one of you. You have made writing this book an exciting adventure.

To my loving and supportive husband, for the illustrations of the book and for always challenging me to write at my best and to take this book to another level.

I am grateful for the services and works of my beautiful editor, Qat Wanders of Wandering Words Media/ https://www.qatwanders.com, my wonderful formatter, Jen Henderson of Wild Words Formatting Services/ http://www.wildwordsformatting.com and an awesome book cover designer, Les, who have all done excellent jobs in making this book possible. Thank you, too, to my talented makeup artist, Ferdinand Moncada for always making me look and feel beautiful in my profile photo.

To my incredible launch team, I am inspired by each one of you, and I am always touched by your support, a million thanks again and again.

To SPS, the Self-Publishing School that taught me to become a self-published author. I am in gratitude to all the staff.

Thank you all so very much from my heart and soul.

ABOUT THE AUTHOR

Elsa Mendoza is a Certified Community Life Coach who has a passion for uplifting, empowering, encouraging, motivating, inspiring and helping others to find their passion in life. She helps people identify their strengths and potentials, and change the mindset and old paradigms for a better life and relationship to self and others. Her motivation in doing so is her survival from a harsh family environment during her childhood until her early 20's and overcoming a rare disease that almost took her life.

She believes in the power of the human mind, its thoughts and the laws of the universe. She is always curious, a thinker and a seeker and confident in the power of humanity and the possibility of a much better world where oneness exists.

Elsa is well traveled, has lived in different countries and has interacted with several nationalities, been exposed to different lifestyles, cultures, and religions, and has seen what humanity has to offer, thus her inspirations for writing this book.

She holds a Masters of Science Degree in International Business at California International University where she has helped small companies thrive in operations and sales. In her free time, she volunteers at Long Beach Rescue Mission. She loves reading, watching movies, plays, concerts, and traveling with her husband.

ALSO BY ELSA MENDOZA

Please check her
Amazon page for latest update:

https://www.amazon.com/
Elsa-Mendoza/e/B071K4XBYQ/

CONNECT WITH THE AUTHOR

Email: elsa@changecreateevolve.com

Follow her on:

https://www.facebook.com/Change.Create.Evolve/

http://elsa.changecreateevolve.com

https://www.instagram.com/your_coach_elsa/

https://twitter.com/Lsavm

https://www.amazon.com/Elsa-Mendoza/e/B071K4XBYQ

https://www.goodreads.com/author/show/16945935.Elsa_Mendoza

https://partners.bookbub.com/authors/4402533/edit

https://www.pinterest.com/elsav_mendoza/boards/

RESOURCES

BOOKS:

The Complete Conversations With God An uncommon dialogue, Gift Edition by Neale Donald Walsch

The Power of Your Subconscious Mind and other Works by Joseph Murphy

The Untethered Soul: The Journey Beyond Yourself by Michael A. Singer

The First and Last Freedom by J. Krishnamurti

You Can Quote Me On This Words to Empower You and Awaken Your Consciousness, by Elsa Mendoza

Wake Up Humanity Poems About You and Me by Elsa Mendoza

ARTICLES:

ONLINE

A letter from Albert Einstein to his daughter on: The Universal Force of Love published by Monoset
https://monoset.com/blogs/journal/a-letter-from-

albert-einstein-to-his-daughter-on-the-universal-force-of-love

What is the Universe Made of? – published by European Space Agency
https://www.esa.int/Our_Activities/Space_Science/Extreme_space/What_is_the_Universe_made_of

Law of Vibration-Universal Laws Explained – published by Upgrade Reality
http://upgradereality.com/law-of-vibration-universal-laws-explained/

The Universal Energy and Vibration – published by Cosmic Continuum
https://www.youtube.com/watch?v=vqM3TE5TDw8

You are Always Creating your Reality – published by You Are Creators
https://www.youtube.com/watch?v=E4jn6AHbhyo

What is consciousness & where is it? – Deepak Chopra published by Science and Non Duality
https://youtu.be/vXC0RUH1axE

What is consciousness? – Eckhart Tolle published by Manifest Your Visions
https://youtu.be/OXqENKQN4oY

No Joke! How Humor Improves Our Health-According to Science by Christopher D. Connors
https://medium.com/the-mission/no-joke-how-humor-improves-our-health-according-to-science-6121a2d302ab

www.ingramcontent.com/pod-product-compliance
Lightning Source LLC
Chambersburg PA
CBHW051829160426
43209CB00006B/1096